GOD BLESS AND
LOVE YOU ... ENJOY!

Chyl K. Warm

Counterfeit COUNTRY Queen Dreams

Cheryl K. Warner

Illustrated by Ashley Teets

Counterfeit County Queen Dreams

by Cheryl K. Warner

illustrated by Ashley Teets

First Printing, 2017

ISBN Hard Cover 978-0-9981977-0-8
Paperback 978-0-9981977-1-5
EBook 978-0-9981977-2-2

PRINTED IN THE UNITED STATES OF AMERICA

All of you are my heroes...I'm grateful, blessed and inspired by you

My Heavenly Father who makes all things possible

Dave, the love of my life

My beloved children, David, Natalie, Tiffany and grandsons,
Jake, Jordan, Alex and Brandon

Mother, Daddy and Barbie

Doll, Hey You and Susie

Jackie, Butch, Shawn, Ray and my extended family

My talented producer, keyboardist and friend, Jay

My amazing mentor, John and his wife, Kei

My second-to-none team and friends, Brenda, Gary, Sherry, Tommy

Howie and his team, Alex, Sam, Scotty

My fabulous DJ friends, all in radio and my talented video producer, Frans

My business associates and friends (Steve, Warren, Marcie, Sewell, Betty, Naomi,
Charlie, Linda, David), producers, musicians, singers, engineers

My JCP family, especially Angela, Amanda, David, Gail and Brittany

My dear music/personal friends and fans, Facebook and Twitter friends

My talented illustrator and friends, Ashley and her mom, Cathy

4

Once upon a time, there lived a happy, young girl who had a loving family, with a good mother, father, and sister. They lived in a small city beside the river with close neighbors, family, and friends.

I was that young girl, always smiling, looking for the bright side of things, and always dreaming, even though often things were difficult for my family. But there was plenty of love coming my way, along with life's teachings about believing in Jesus and teachings about being a loving, good person, along with lots of encouragement from my parents to explore and follow my dreams.

Even though money was tight, our mother always found a way to pay for dancing lessons for my sister and me. We were taught every kind of dancing they offered: ballet, toe, tap, baton, and acrobatics.

The lessons were so much fun, and my sister and I were told that we were naturally talented, so we just kept dancing throughout our school years. At an early age, we even formed a vocal trio for singing and actually performed quite a lot.

I wanted to go to a university to study the arts, but my father guided my path into a nursing career to become a registered nurse.

12

That was a good thing because I was able to help so many people. I enjoyed being a nurse, doing my best to make everyone feel better.

That's how I met my handsome prince charming, whom I married. He is such a wonderful man and is an engineer.

We have been so happy together and have been blessed to have three beautiful children: a son and two daughters...

...and we have also been blessed to have four grandsons. They constantly amaze us, always making us smile while filling our hearts with their very special kind of love.

My husband and children have filled my life so completely and lovingly. All of this was my biggest dream in life: to have a happy family and become a wife and mother and, now, a grandmother.

After writing songs, I was able to reach for more of my childhood dreams, like becoming a recording artist and a musical entertainer.

Many wonderful people who have been my friends and other people that I met along my journey helped me to become very successful with my singing and writing of many songs.

One of my most successful songs is called "Counterfeit Country Queen." It's a story about my feeling like I'm a true country music artist, and even many people who don't like country music have become fans of my style of country music.

I love to make people happy with my recordings, and when I have the opportunity to sing live for them on stage, I feel a wonderful connection, an exchange of love wherever I sing for people.

And I love it when people tell me that there is "nothing counterfeit" about me at all, that I'm "real," and that they are glad I kept reaching for my dreams and remained true to who I am.

So, I hope that you'll always remember to believe in Jesus and in yourself and in your dreams. Don't let anything ever stop you from becoming whom you would like to be—anything you dream is possible.